AF569966

Art Books

The empty pages

(except this)

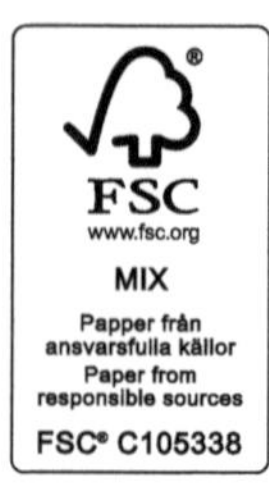

(and this)

Förlag: BoD – Books on Demand, Stockholm, Sverige
Tryck: BoD – Books on Demand, Norderstedt, Tyskland

ISBN: 978-91-8007-717-0

Oh no!

This page is not empty!

Never mind!

Carry on!

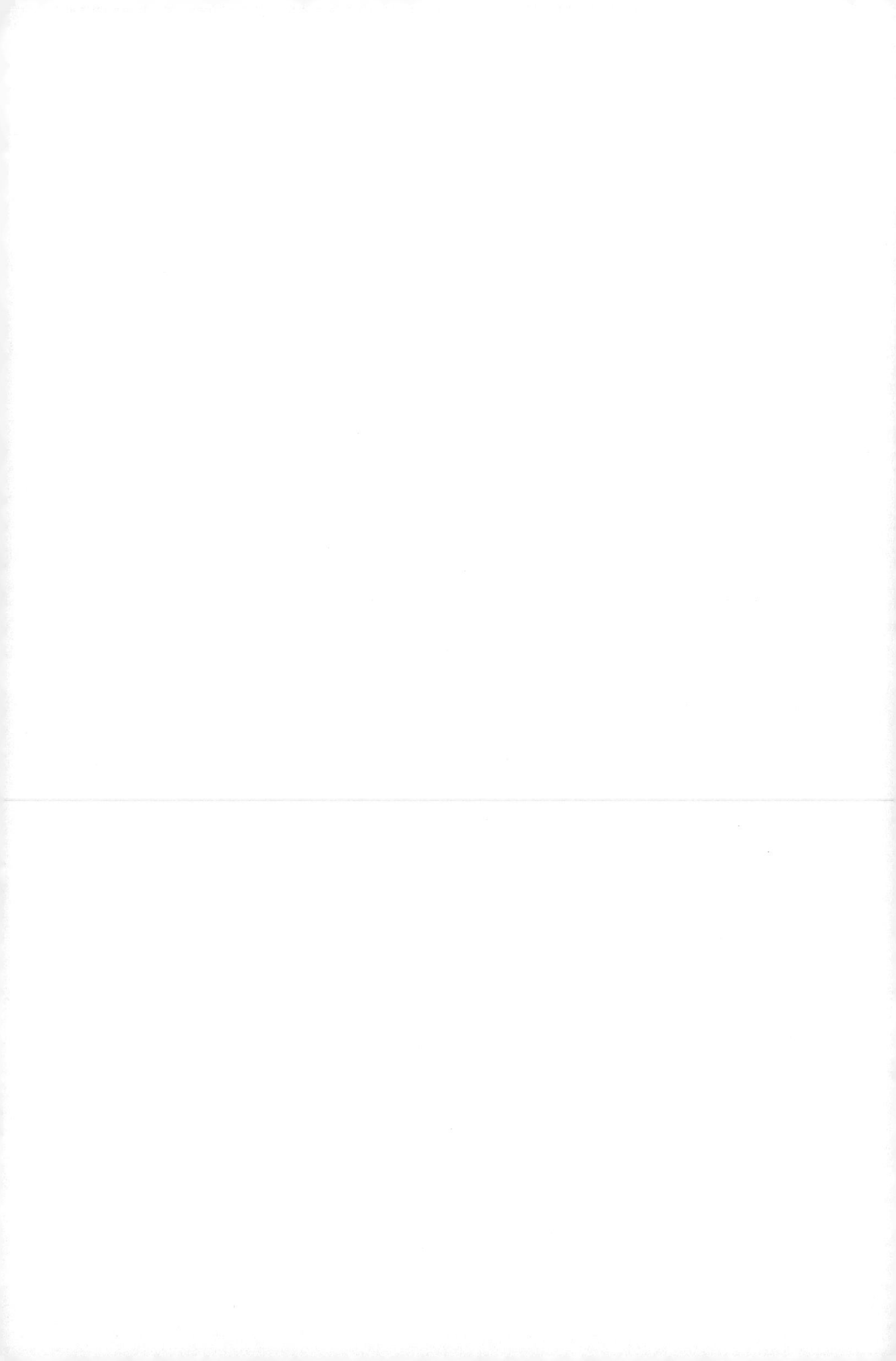

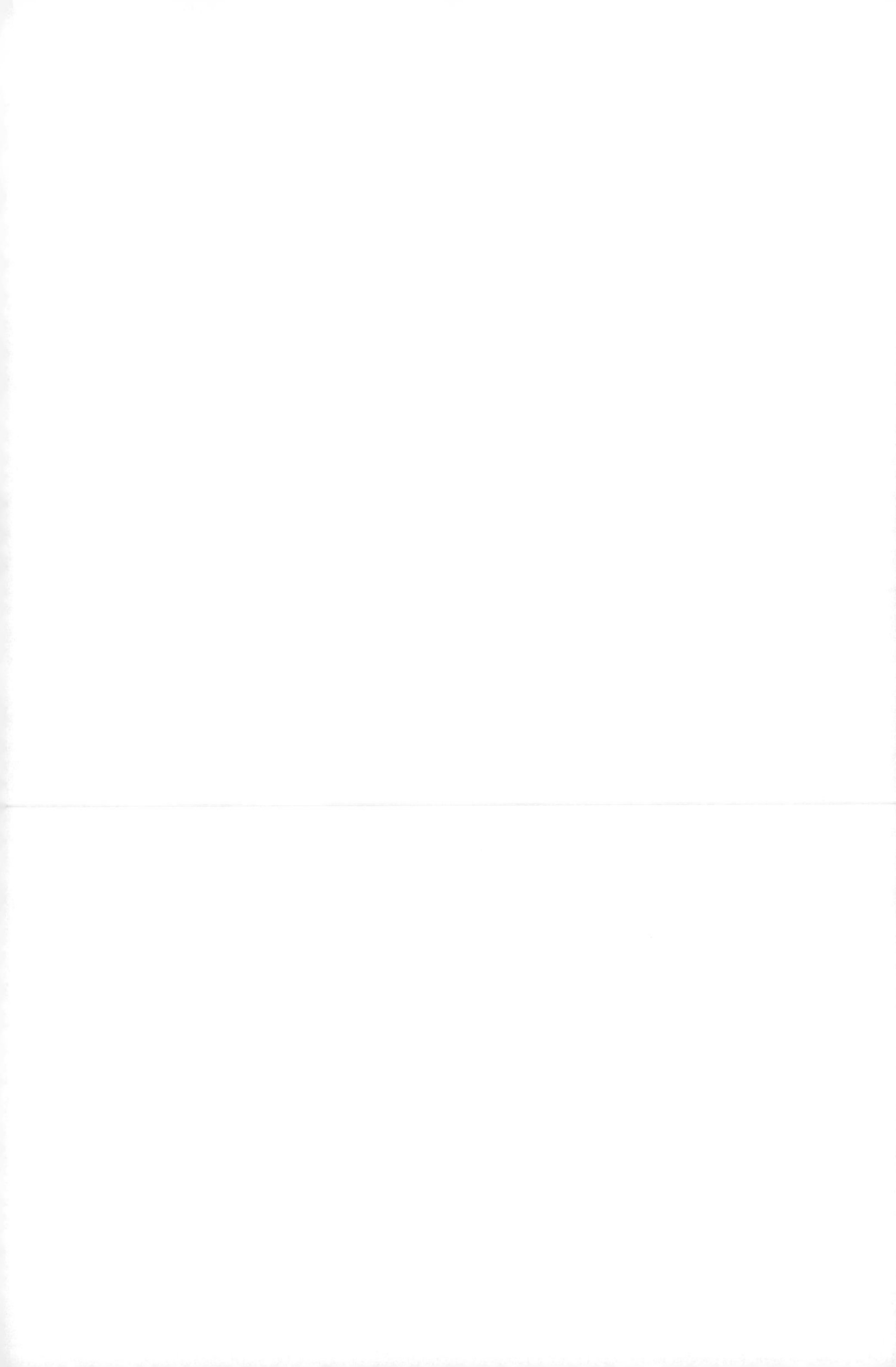

Yet another not empty page!

Perhaps this book should be called:

"The almost empty pages"!?

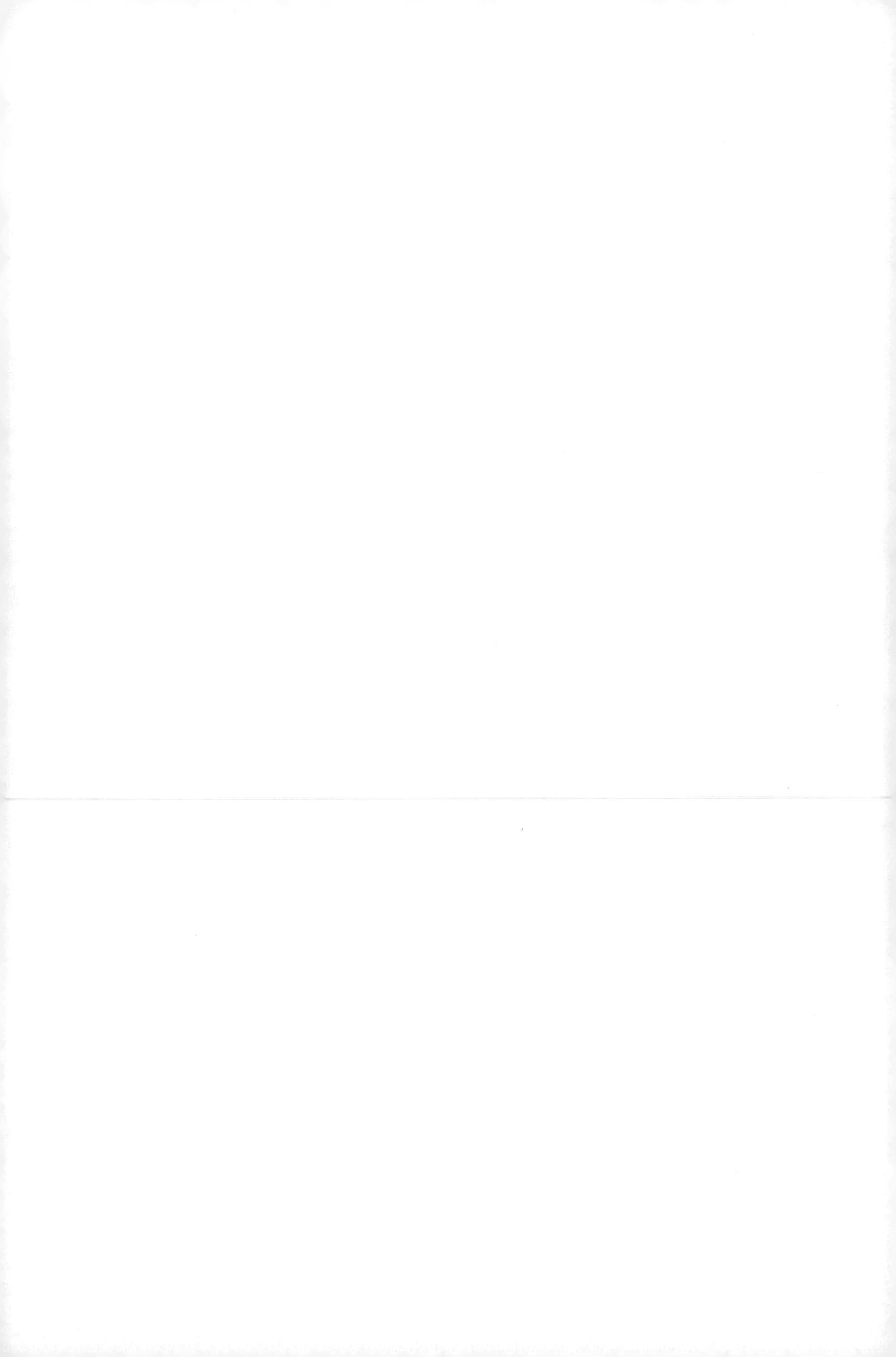

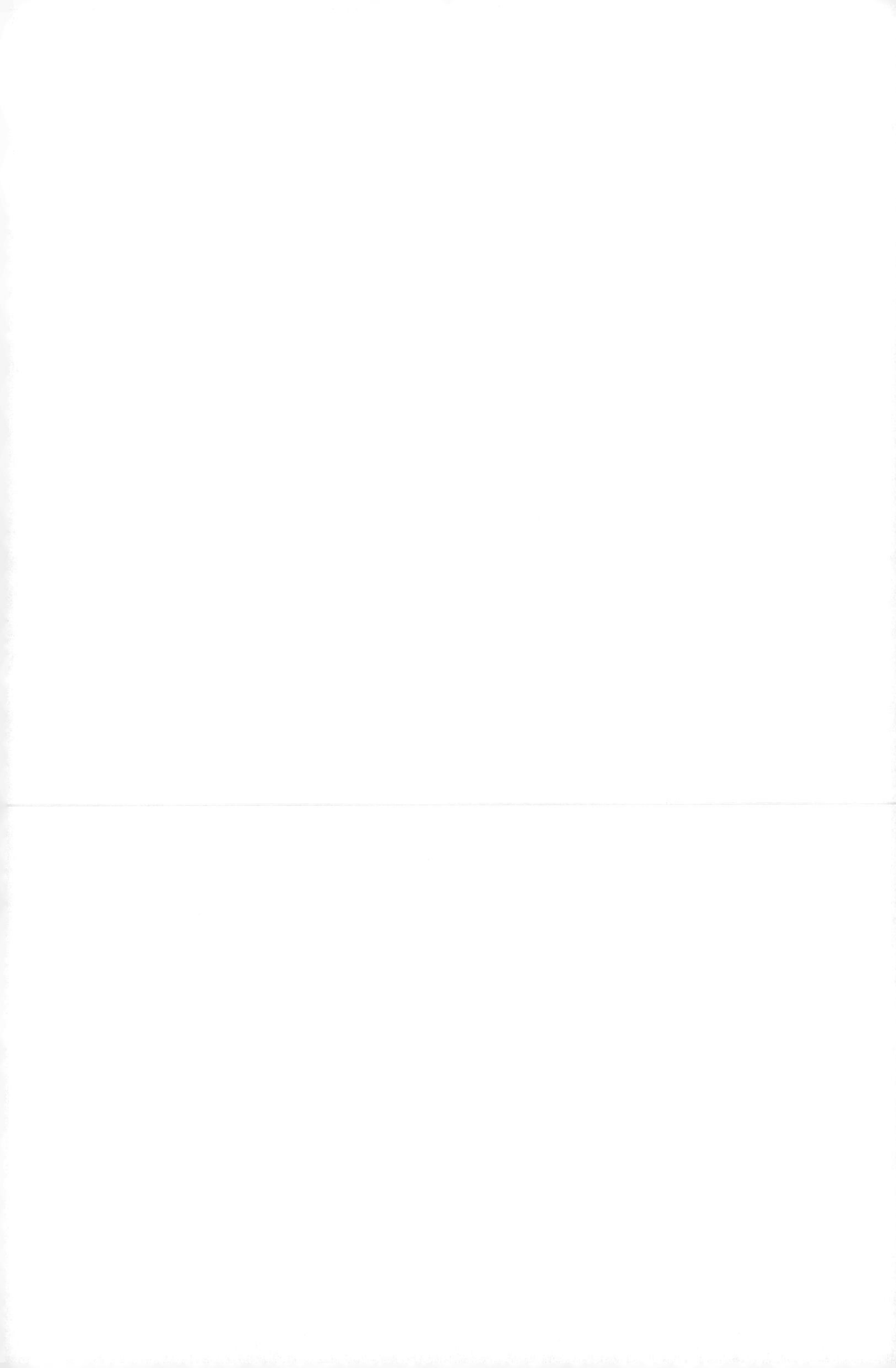

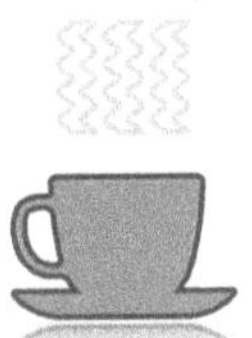